HOW TO DESIGN THE WORLD'S BEST

SPACE STATION

IN 10 SIMPLE STEPS

PAUL MASON

WAYLAND
www.waylandbooks.co.uk

First published in Great Britain in 2016 by Wayland

Copyright © Hodder and Stoughton Limited, 2016

Editor: Nicola Edwards
Design: Kevin Knight

Artwork by Tim Hutchinson

ISBN: 978 0 7502 9999 2
10 9 8 7 6 5 4 3 2 1

MIX
Paper from
responsible sources
FSC® C104740
FSC
www.fsc.org

Wayland, an imprint of
Hachette Children's Group
Part of Hodder and Stoughton
Carmelite House
50 Victoria Embankment
London EC4Y 0DZ

An Hachette UK Company
www.hachette.co.uk
www.hachettechildrens.co.uk

Printed and bound in China

Picture acknowledgements:
All photographs courtesy of NASA except for
p12 NASA/MSFC Historical Archives; p25 Shutterstock

Every attempt has been made to clear copyright.
Should there be any inadvertent omission,
please apply to the publisher for rectification.

The website addresses (URLs) included in this book were valid
at the time of going to press. However, it is possible that
contents or addresses may have changed since the publication
of this book. No responsibility for any such changes can be
accepted by either the author or the Publisher.

CONTENTS

DESIGNING THE WORLD'S BEST SPACE STATION

Pick a good night, with a clear sky, and go outside. If you have timed it right (find out which are the good nights at https://spotthestation.nasa.gov/sightings/), you will see a bright light whizzing across the sky. It takes just a few minutes to appear, get brighter, fade, and then disappear. It's a space station passing by.

Imagine what it would be like up there. What would you need, to be able to live in space?

Now imagine designing you own space station. How would you go about it?

DESIGNING SPACE STATIONS... OR ANYTHING!

Designing a space station is like designing almost anything else. First, you make a sketch or plan. This has to match the design brief, the list of things your design has to be able to do.

On a space station, for example, the design brief might include things like, 'provide sleeping space' and 'give astronauts somewhere to wash'.

Next, you look at every part of the design, asking yourself some crucial questions:
• Does it fit the design brief?
• Can it actually be built? (This is really two questions: is it possible, and can we afford it?)
• Is there a better way of achieving the same thing?

Depending on the answers, the original design can be adapted, or even changed completely.

If you find the thought of living up in space inspiring, how about trying to design the best space station ever?

Space stations come in lots of different shapes.

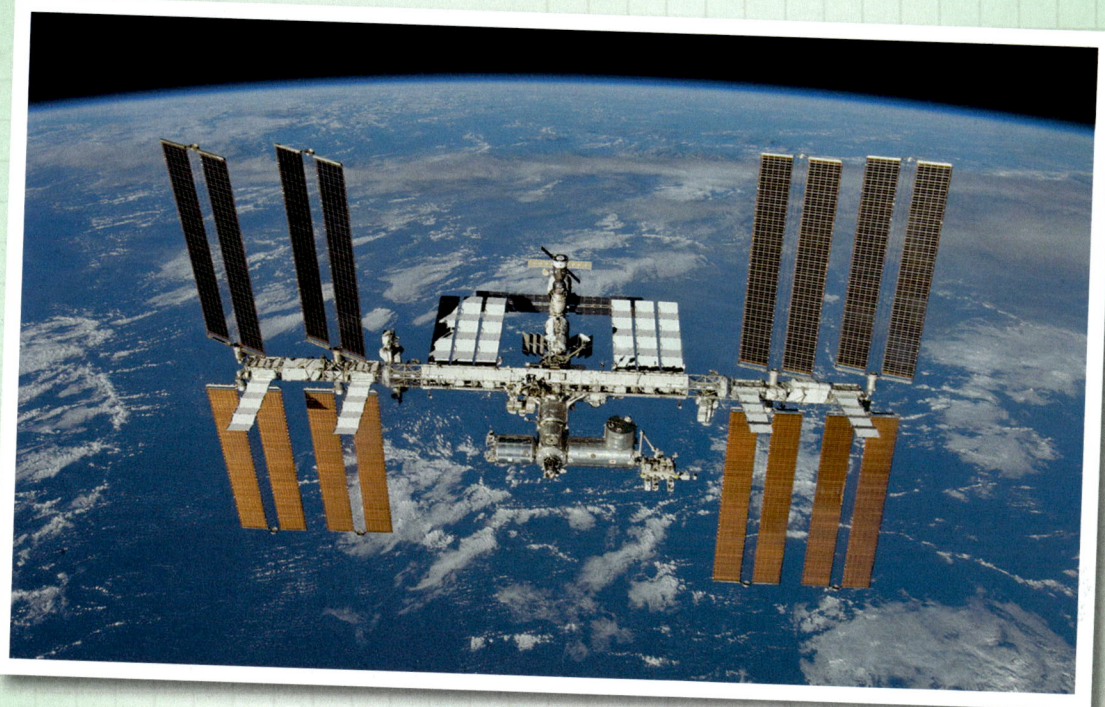

This space station gets power from long strips of solar panels.

SPACE-STATION RESEARCH

Designers usually base their designs partly on their own experience. For this job, though, you are probably going to have to rely on research! So where could you find out about space stations?

1) The Internet

The Internet contains lots of information about space. Not all of it is reliable, so it is important to use trustworthy websites. The best Internet researchers also use more than one search engine. Alternatives to Google include yippy.com and duckduckgo.com (you can find out more about these on page 31).

2) Books

People have been designing (but not building) space stations since the 1900s. A visit to a library could unearth some ideas even the Internet has not yet recorded.

Research Note

These are some clues that a website can be trusted:

• The information contains facts, not opinions. For example:

'The First World War started when Austria-Hungary declared war on Serbia'; not, 'The war started because of German aggression.'

• The site is clear, with no spelling or grammatical mistakes.

• Its address ends with .org, .edu or .gov – these usually mean it is run by the government or an organisation, such as a museum.

WHAT IS THE SPACE STATION FOR?

The first thing a designer asks when they start a new job is: 'What is this thing going to be used for?'. People will be living aboard the space station, but it is not just a guest house with fantastic views! It will also be used for other purposes.

USES FOR THE SPACE STATION

The space station's main use is going to be for scientific research. Scientists want to know whether humans can survive in space for long periods of time. Space is very different from Earth: there is no air and practically no gravity. If humans are ever to make long-distance space journeys, or even live in space, the effects of being up there have to be studied and understood.

Space travellers of the future would also need reliable spacecraft. These will have to last a long time, because journeys through space take many years. The craft will have to be self-powered, because there are no petrol stations in space! And they will need to provide the passengers with food and drink, because there are no supermarkets, either.

The space station could provide ideas for how all of these things can be achieved. So the design needs to include a lab for science experiments and equipment.

Experimenting with gravity inside a specially built laboratory.

MAKING THE SPACE STATION HABITABLE

If humans are going to live aboard for weeks, or even months, the space station has to be habitable. It needs to be a bit like a hotel, providing everything the guests need. (And if space tourism ever really takes off, it might have to work as an actual hotel.)

As designer, you will have to work out the human needs of the space station's inhabitants, and make sure they are provided for in your design.

It's a slightly cramped dining hall! Astronauts having lunch inside the International Space Station.

WORK IT OUT!

Draw up a checklist of the things people do throughout the day. You can use this list to make sure your design contains everything people need.

Start by making a list of everything you and your family do for 24 hours. Separate out all the different activities – for example, 'Go to the toilet' can actually describe two activities. You need to list both!

Separate the essential and non-essential activities. For example, if your list has, '16.00–16.30: Swimming lessons', you can mark that as non essential. A swimming pool will not have to be included in the space station's design.

Test your ideas against the list on page 31.

The shape is familiar – but look closer and you'll see this is a toilet with a difference.

DRAW OUT A DREAM DESIGN

You have researched information about space stations. You have found out what this space station is going to be used for. You can work out the needs of the people who will be living aboard it. It is time to sketch out your first design.

READY FOR REVISIONS

No design is ever perfect first go. Little changes and improvements are always needed, whether you are designing a chair or an office building. In this first sketch, you draw a dream design. You can sketch whatever you want – as long as it fits the design brief.

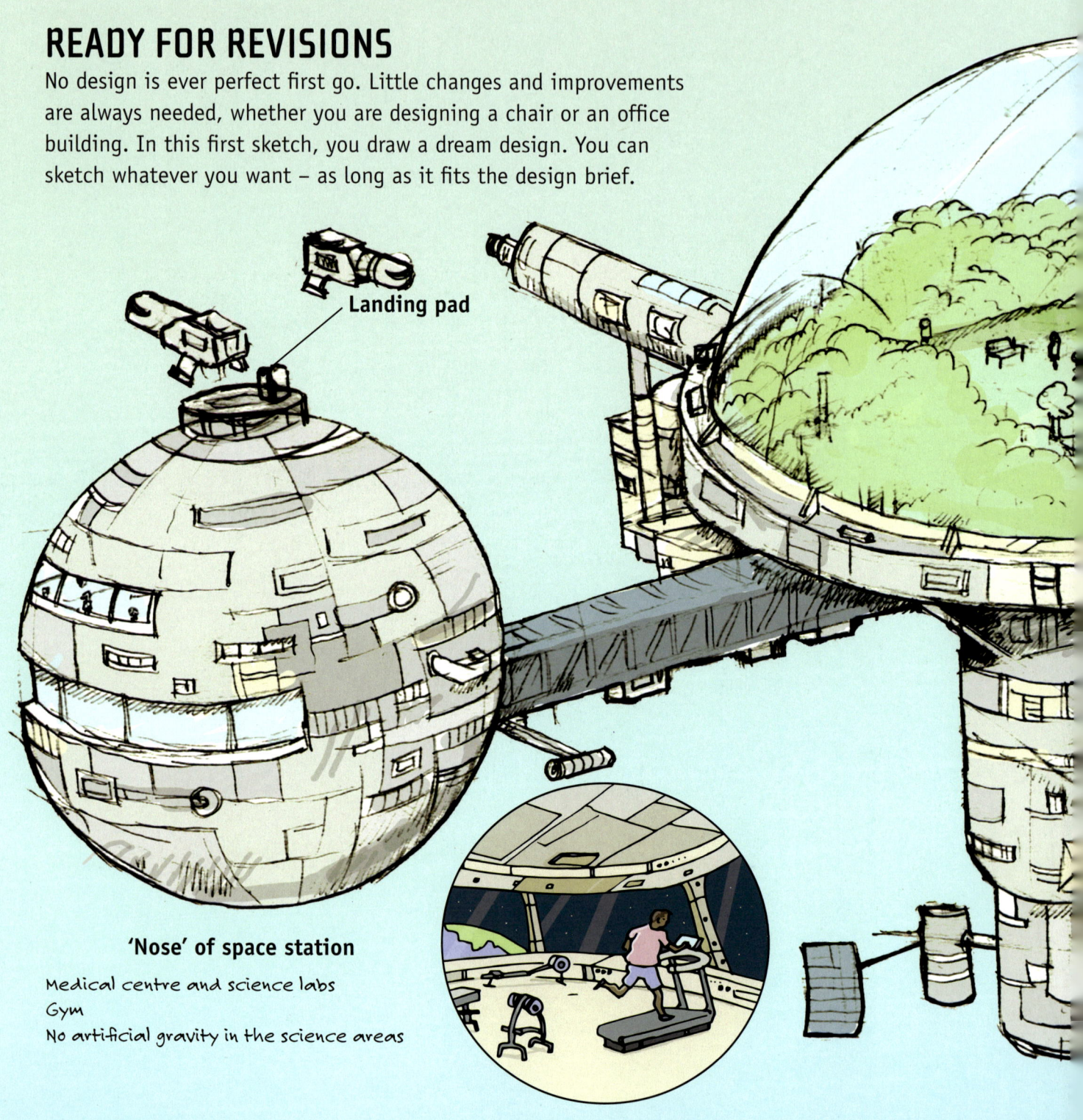

Landing pad

'Nose' of space station

Medical centre and science labs
Gym
No artificial gravity in the science areas

Central leisure area

Grass area for football and other games

Trees and plants turn carbon dioxide (from human breath) into oxygen

Guest sleeping quarters
For space tourists, these bedrooms will be like those on a cruise liner

Permanent sleeping quarters
Long-term residents will share bunk rooms

Restaurant

Nuclear fusion reactor
Provides power for artificial gravity aboard the space station

WORK IT OUT!

Look at the information on pages 6 and 7, plus your results from the WORK IT OUT! panel on page 7. Use these to make two lists.

The first list is things the space station has to have. The second list is things it would be good to include, but which are not essential. The lists could start like this:

Essential	Non essential
Science lab	Play area
Washing facilities	Football pitch

The design on these pages is based on similar lists. (You can check your ideas on page 31.)

CHECK THE CONSTRUCTION COSTS

You now have a dream design for the best space station ever.
The next step is to work out whether it can actually be built!
If it can, every part of the design will then have to be
examined, to see if it works and whether it could be improved.

BUILD COSTS

'Build costs' are exactly what they sound like:
the costs of building something. They include
transport, materials and labour. Before you
take your space-station design any further,
you need to work out roughly how much it
will cost. A good starting place would be to
discover the amount of money that was spent
on other space stations.

Research Note

The first working space station was Russia's
Salyut. *Salyut* was built on Earth, before being
launched into orbit in 1971 without anyone
aboard. Later, the crew used a rocket to reach
the space station. They lived there for just
over three weeks.

Later space stations, such as *Mir* and the
International Space Station, were built in
space. They were designed so that extra
sections could be added to the design later.

The Russian Mir space station above
Earth. Mir was in orbit for 15 years.

The USA's Skylab was launched in 1973.

WORK IT OUT!

The three most famous space stations are the United States' *Skylab*, Russia's *Mir*, and today's *International Space Station*.

Use these numbers to work out how much each space station cost to build per kg (the costs include transport of materials and have been adjusted to current values):

Space station	Estimated build cost	Weight
Skylab (1973–79)	US$10 billion	100,000kg
Mir (1986–2001)	US$5.6 billion	100,000kg
International Space Station (1998–present)	US$100 billion	391,000kg

You can check your answers on page 31.

WHAT WILL THE DREAM DESIGN COST?

As designer, you need to work out how much your dream space station would cost to build. You can estimate this by comparing it to the International Space Station (usually called *ISS*). This is the most recent space station, and it cost US$255,754 per kg. The dream design is forecast to weigh 700,000kg, which is...
(700,000 x 255,754 = 179,027,800,000)
... Nearly US$180 billion!

Unfortunately, a financial crisis has happened since planning started. These days, no one can afford to spend US$180 billion on a space station. The new budget is US$110 billion (which is still quite a lot of money...). This means the station can be roughly 400,000kg in weight. It will need to be smaller and simpler than the original design.

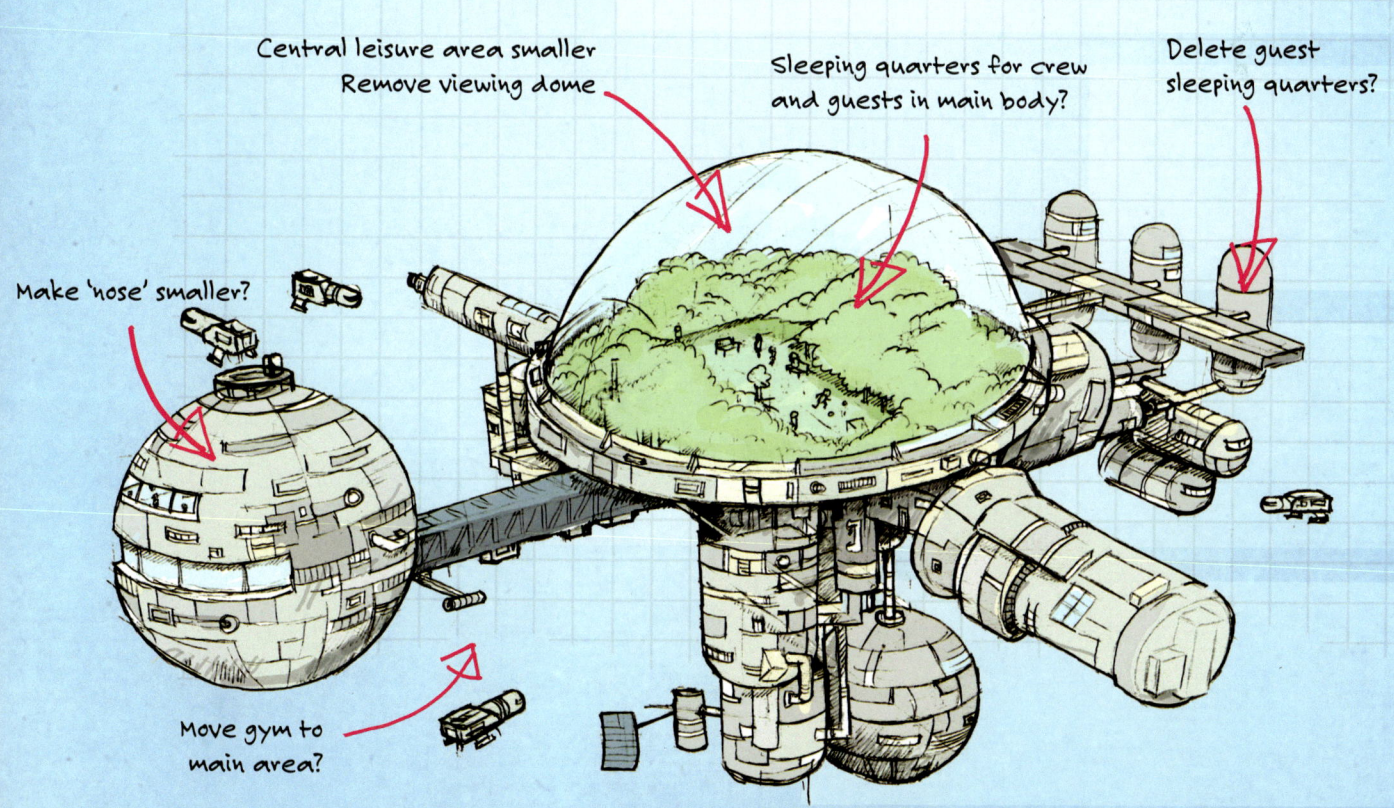

Central leisure area smaller
Remove viewing dome

Sleeping quarters for crew and guests in main body?

Delete guest sleeping quarters?

Make 'nose' smaller?

Move gym to main area?

POWER YOUR SPACE STATION

The original plan was for the space station's main energy source to be nuclear fusion. This energy would power the space station's artificial gravity (except in the science lab, where no gravity is wanted). This sounds good – but there are two quite big problems... 1) Nuclear fusion doesn't exist 2) Nor does an artificial-gravity machine.

POSSIBLE CHANGES
Solutions to two problems are now needed:

1) Where will the space station get its power?
The answer to this is simple. The space station will spend half its time in bright sunlight. Installing solar panels would provide it with plenty of energy.

Werner von Braun's design for a space station, drawn in 1952. Von Braun also designed the USA's Saturn space rockets.

WORK IT OUT!

Scientists have calculated that the space station's computers, laboratories and life-support systems will use between 75 and 90 kilowatts of energy each day.

For safety, the solar panels need to be able to provide a little more energy than is actually needed. An additional 10–15% is needed.

If one solar panel can provide 12.9 kilowatts of energy, how many solar panels does the space station need?

You can check your answer on page 31.

2) Can there be gravity aboard the space station?
Since gravity-machines have not yet been invented, the short answer is, 'No'. But there is a way of making it feel as though there is gravity on the space station.

To demonstrate, imagine an old plastic bucket filled with water and with half a metre of strong rope tied to the handle. If you were to swing the bucket round and round fast enough, no water would spill out – even when the bucket was upside-down.

Now imagine a space station circling like the bucket. The people on board would be held in place in the same way as the water.

The trouble is, experts have worked out that to produce a force of 1 g, the distance from the centre to the edge would have to be 224m. If the space station was wheel-shaped like the one shown on page 12, it would be nearly half a kilometre across. The design is meant to be getting smaller, not growing!

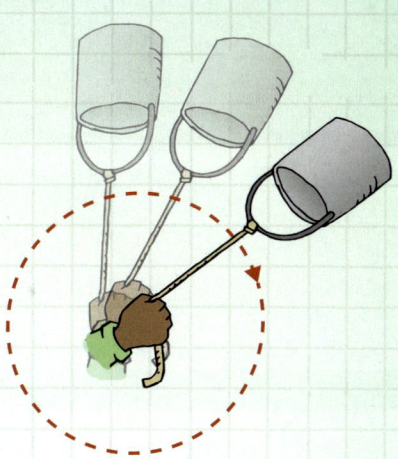

THE FINAL DESIGN

The final design is for the space station to have eight solar panels, and no artificial gravity at all. After all, part of the special space experience is floating around! This is the simplest and least expensive option.

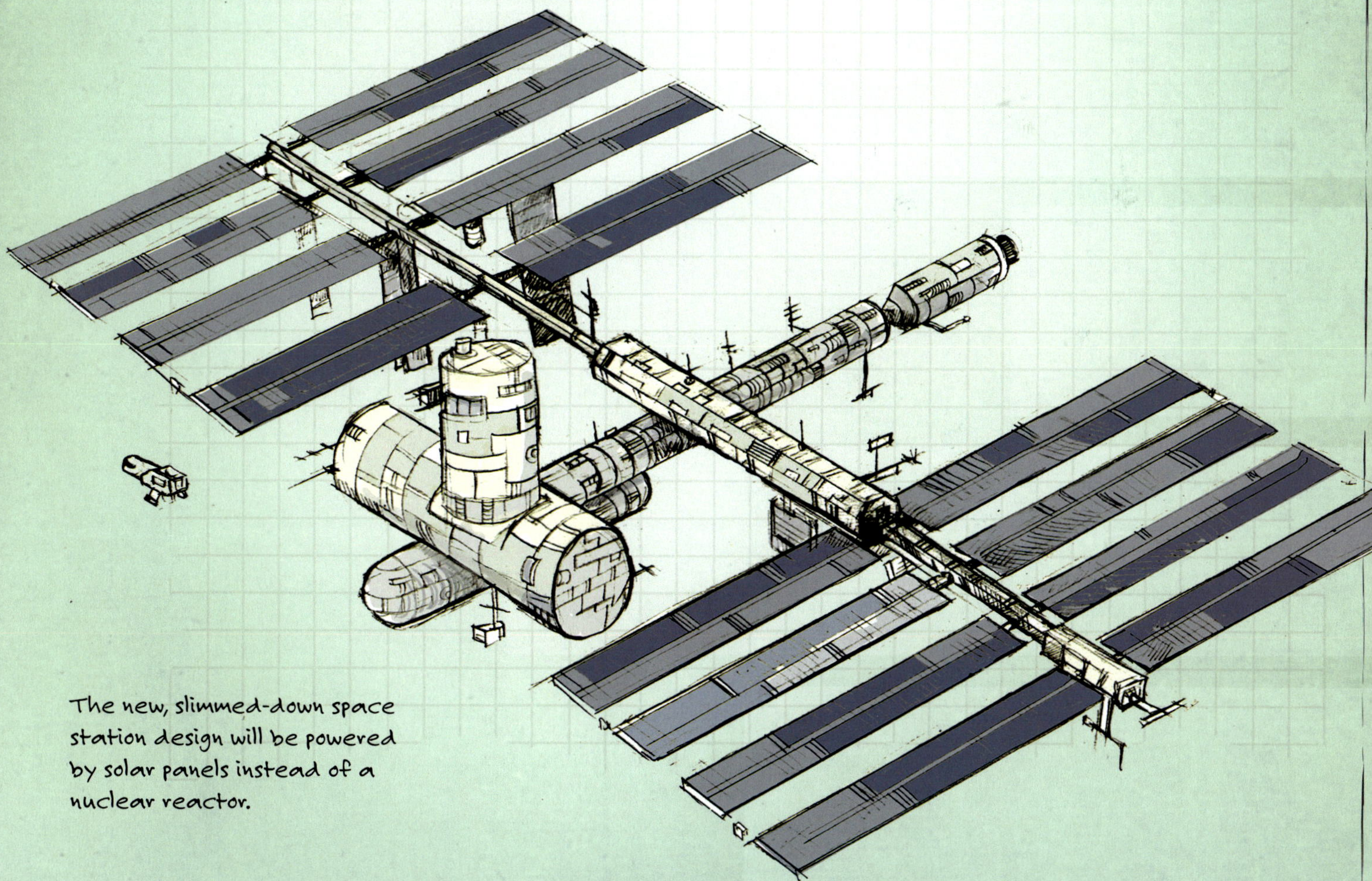

The new, slimmed-down space station design will be powered by solar panels instead of a nuclear reactor.

DESIGN THE FRONT DOOR

To build the space station, some of the workers will have to work outside. This is called a space walk or EVA. Later, the crew might also have to do EVAs to make repairs if the station is damaged. So that they can do this, the space station needs a door.

INSIDE TO OUTSIDE

Designing just an ordinary door would be no good. Opening it would let all the air inside the space station escape into space. The crew needs a way of getting out without this happening.

Research Note

Space is a dangerous and hostile place:

• There is no air to breathe.

• Temperatures range from -155°C to 121°C.

• Sunlight is strong enough to cause blindness.

• Space dust travelling at hundreds of kilometres per hour can cause serious damage.

• Radiation (invisible rays) can cause sickness and even death in living things.

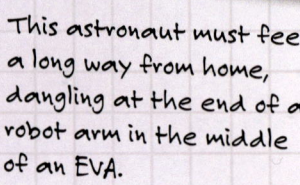

This astronaut must feel a long way from home, dangling at the end of a robot arm in the middle of an EVA.

These astronauts have finished their EVA and are going back inside.

WORK IT OUT!

Research the ways people move from a safe environment into a hostile one. For example, how do divers leave a submarine in order to get out into the undersea world?

Could any of the designs you have found be used as a way of getting in and out of the space station?

Check your thinking on page 31.

WORK IT OUT!

Astronauts doing an EVA have to wear two pairs of gloves, plus a bulky space suit. How tricky does this make work for them?

To find out, you need four people with two pairs of gloves each, plus a jigsaw puzzle. Write A on the back of every outside piece of the puzzle, and B on the back of every inside piece.

One pair of players gets all the As, the other gets all the Bs. The A players leave their 'base' and move to an imaginary 'work zone'. Wearing two pairs of gloves each (like an astronaut in a space suit), they assemble the outside edge of the jigsaw puzzle.

When the A players return to 'base', the B players leave to assemble the inside part of the jigsaw puzzle.

THE FINAL DESIGN

The space station will be fitted with an 'airlock' system. Before using the airlock system, crew members help the astronaut to put on a space suit. The airlock system works like this:

1) The astronaut goes through the inner door. The door between the inside and the airlock is closed.
2) When they are ready, the astronauts open the door to the outside, and the air rushes out!
3) When it is time to come back inside, everything works in reverse.

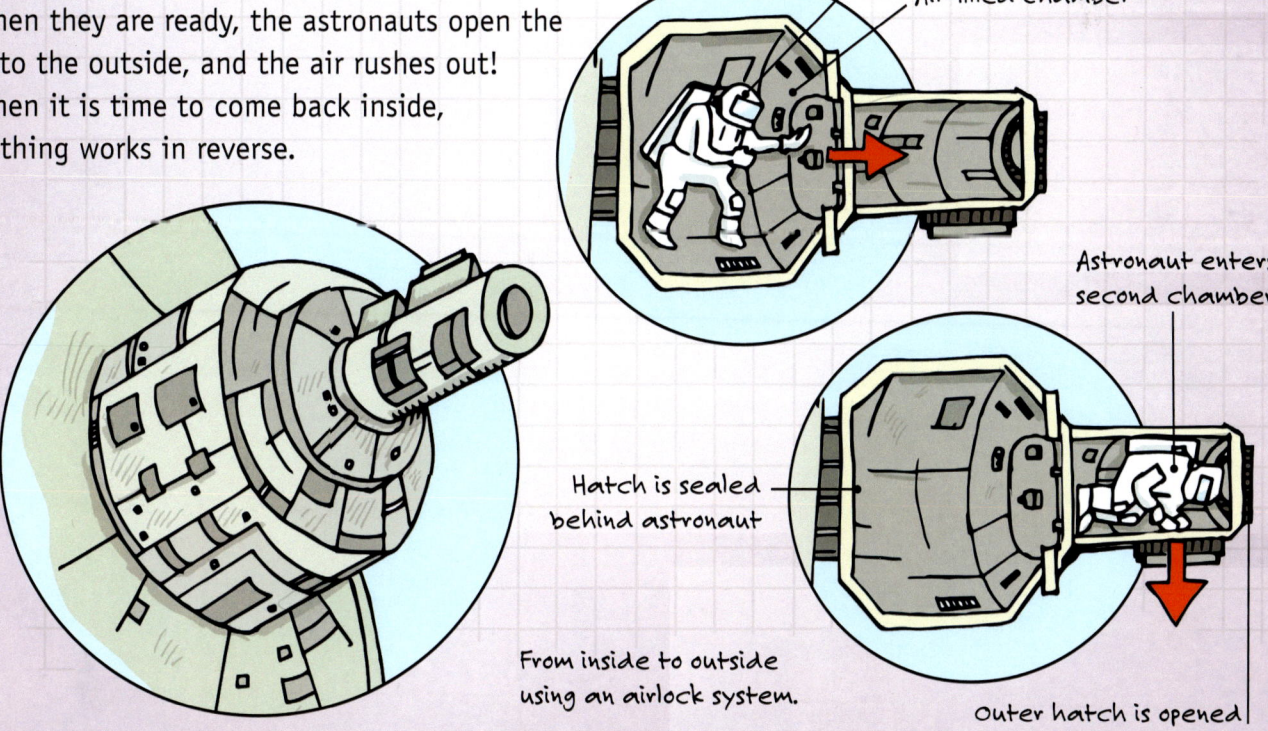

Astronaut prepares for EVA

Air-filled chamber

Astronaut enters second chamber

Hatch is sealed behind astronaut

Outer hatch is opened

From inside to outside using an airlock system.

MOVE THE SPACE STATION ABOUT

To stay at the same height, the space station needs to be travelling around the Earth at a constant speed. If it slows down, it drops slowly back towards Earth. But there is a problem. The space station will be constantly slowed down by space dust, being hit by objects such as micrometeoroids, and so on.

MOVING IN SPACE

Experts have worked out that in one year, the space station would slow down so much that it would fall over 2km. Unless it can regularly be moved higher, it will eventually crash back to Earth.

Being able to move about in space would also help the space station avoid damaging crashes. Colliding with a piece of space junk or a meteoroid (which travel at hundreds of kilometres an hour) would be disastrous.

Research Note

The space station will be in orbit only 400km above the Earth's surface. At that height, Earth's gravity is almost 90% as powerful as down on the surface. So how come the space station will not fall back to Earth?

The answer is that the effect of gravity will be balanced out by another force: the space station's direction of travel.

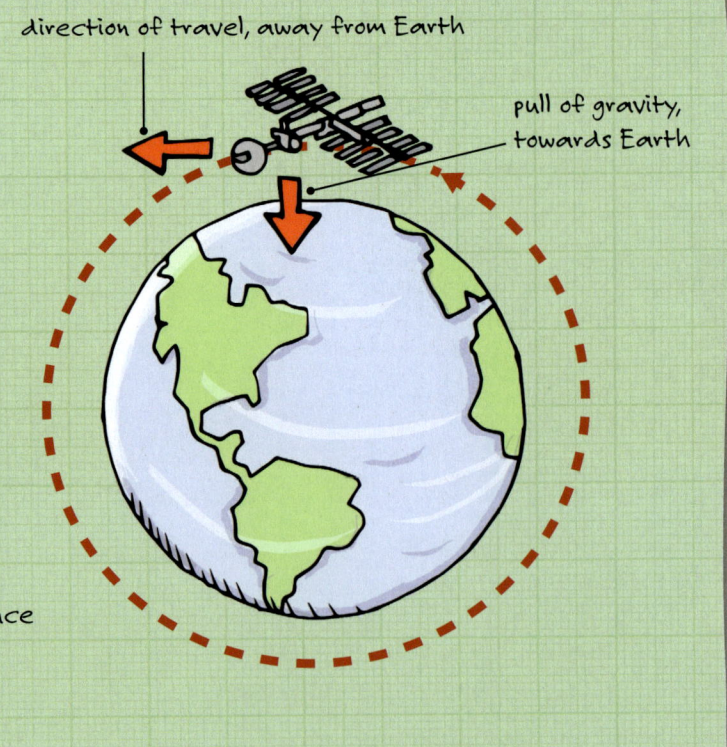

direction of travel, away from Earth

pull of gravity, towards Earth

These two forces balance out to keep the space station in orbit.

WORK IT OUT!

This experiment shows you how the speed at which something is travelling affects the damage it can do.

You need the bottom part of an old shoebox, some tissue paper, a peashooter, and some dried peas. Tape the tissue paper over the shoebox, getting it as flat as possible.

1) Drop a pea on the tissue paper.

2) Turn the shoebox on its side and throw a pea at it.

3) Now fire a pea at the shoebox using the peashooter.

Which caused the most damage? You can check your results on page 31.

THE FINAL DESIGN

The final design is for the space station to be moved in two possible ways.

First, it will be fitted with four small rockets. These will point in different directions, making it possible to move the station small distances.

Second, the places where other spacecraft are attached will be made stronger. That way, their rockets can be used to move the space station.

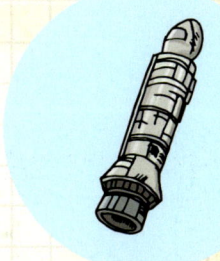

Rockets on each end of each solar-panel arm and at each end of the main body of the space station.

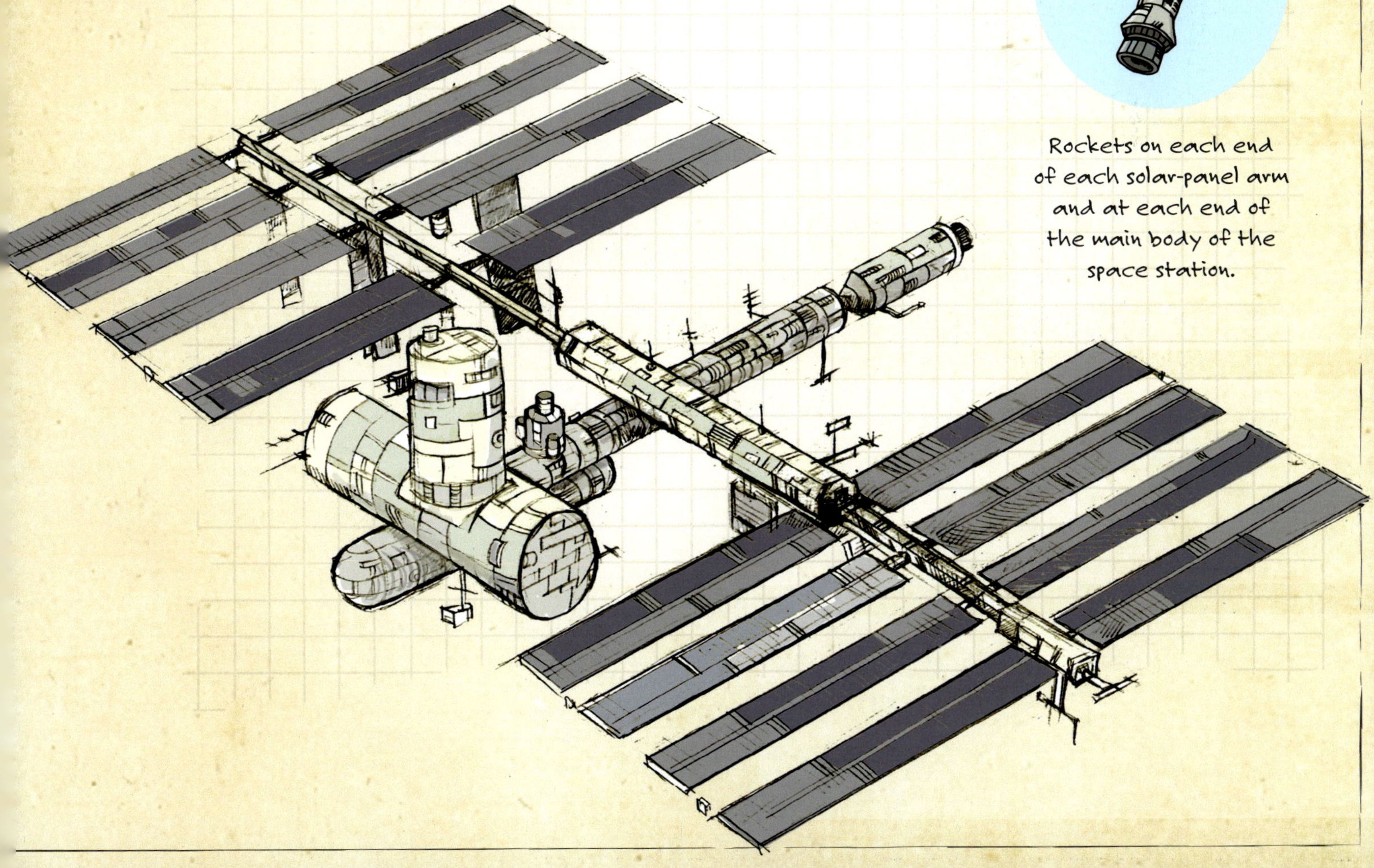

DESIGN A SPACE KITCHEN

The original design had a large dining area, where people could sit and chat while having their meals. Sadly, though, the downsizing of the space station after the financial crisis means there are two big problems with the old design:

Eating without the help of gravity is not as easy as you might think!

Problem 1: Lack of room

The large dome from the original plan has had to be cut from the design. It would have been too expensive to build. The social area will now be much smaller (about the size of an average room) and will not have any viewing windows.

Problem 2: Lack of gravity

Gravy without gravity is no joke! Imagine piling up potatoes without gravity to help keep them in place. And how would you eat ice-cream if it kept floating away?

Research Note

Gravity on the space station is about 90% as strong as it is on Earth. So why does the crew feel there is no gravity aboard?

The space station is trying to travel in a straight line, moving away from Earth. But gravity constantly pulls it down. This means that the space station and its crew are constantly falling back towards Earth.

Everyone on board is like someone falling out of a tree. Gravity is acting on them all the time – but they cannot feel it.

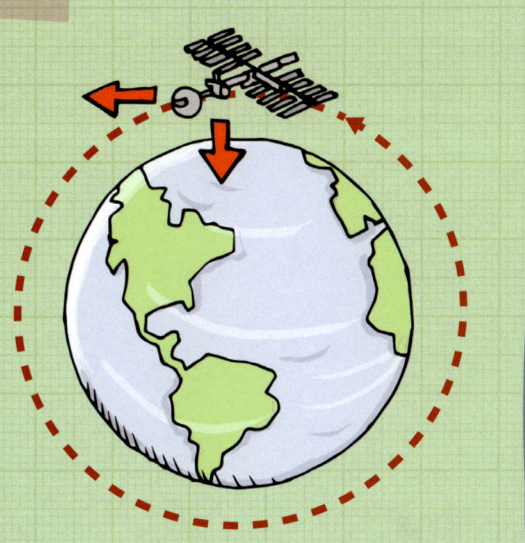

POSSIBLE SOLUTIONS

The first problem is easy to solve. The crew will have to prepare their food and eat in their living space, where they will also relax.

The second problem is more difficult. How can you cook and eat when there is no gravity? In the 1950s, the first astronauts took food in toothpaste tubes. They could squeeze the food (which apparently tasted revolting) into their mouths. For the space station, though, special meals are needed.

WORK IT OUT!

Design a gravity-free version of your favourite lunch for the space station.

All the preparation work must be done inside plastic bags, to stop the parts floating away.

Your lunch can be heated inside an oven, but it cannot go under a grill or on top of a cooker. Those rely on gravity to keep the food in place.

There is no correct answer to this job, but an Internet search for 'Sandra Magnus cooks in space' or 'Heston Blumenthal creates bacon sandwich for Tim Peake' might give you some ideas.

Could fruit juggling become a new space sport? Astronauts Magnus and Kimbrough chase their food around the cabin.

...AND A SPACE BATHROOM

In the original design, there were walk-in shower rooms. The waste water would have been sucked away by artificial gravity, before being recycled. The toilets in the bathrooms would have worked just like toilets back here on Earth. On the new gravity-free space station, this is impossible. As designer, this has given you some challenges.

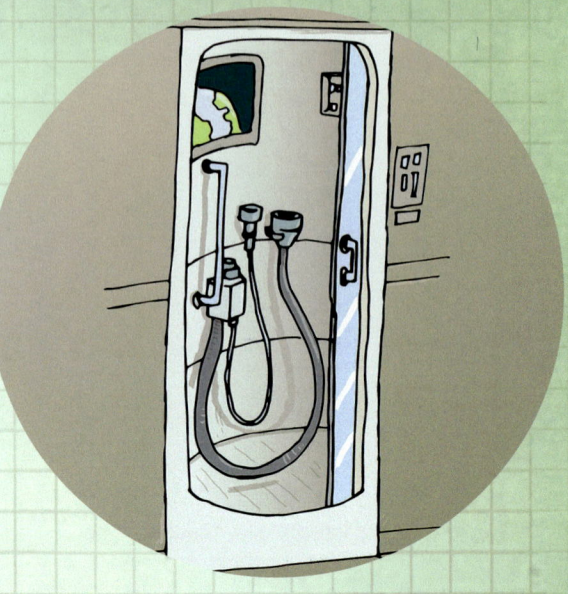

BATHROOM CHALLENGES

How can people shower unless gravity pulls the water off their bodies and down the plughole? And how will they go to the toilet? (It would have been bad enough in the kitchen if some of the ingredients had got loose. In the bathroom it would be VERY unpleasant.)

Showers like the dream design's only work when there is gravity to pull the water downwards. Now the space station does not have gravity, you need to come up with a different way of getting clean!

WORK IT OUT!

Research has shown that liquid waste from the toilet can be recycled as drinking water. Every bit of water aboard the space station will have to be flown up from Earth, so recycling water in this way would be a good idea.

BUT...

The liquid waste cannot be mixed with solid waste. So your job is to sketch a design for a space toilet. It has to:

1) Collect liquids and solids separately

2) Suck the waste away somehow – otherwise it will just float around.

Astronaut Samantha Cristoforetti of the European Space Agency (or ESA) has made two videos showing how the toilets and bathrooms aboard ISS work. To see them and get some ideas for your own design, do an Internet video search for 'ESA *International Space Station* toilet tour' and 'ESA *International Space Station* bathroom tour'.)

Research Note

Human toilet waste can be recycled or used in different ways:

• Liquid waste can be treated and turned into drinking water. (Some experts will tell you that every drop of water you drink was once dinosaur wee, recycled into the Earth's water store. But that's another story.)

• Solid waste can be treated and used as plant fertiliser.

THE FINAL DESIGN

In the final toilet design, liquid waste is sucked gently down a tube, ready to be recycled as drinking water. Solid waste is sucked away into a different container. Unfortunately, anyone who wants to wash will find there are no showers, and definitely no baths! Instead they will have to wipe themselves clean using special towels and soap.

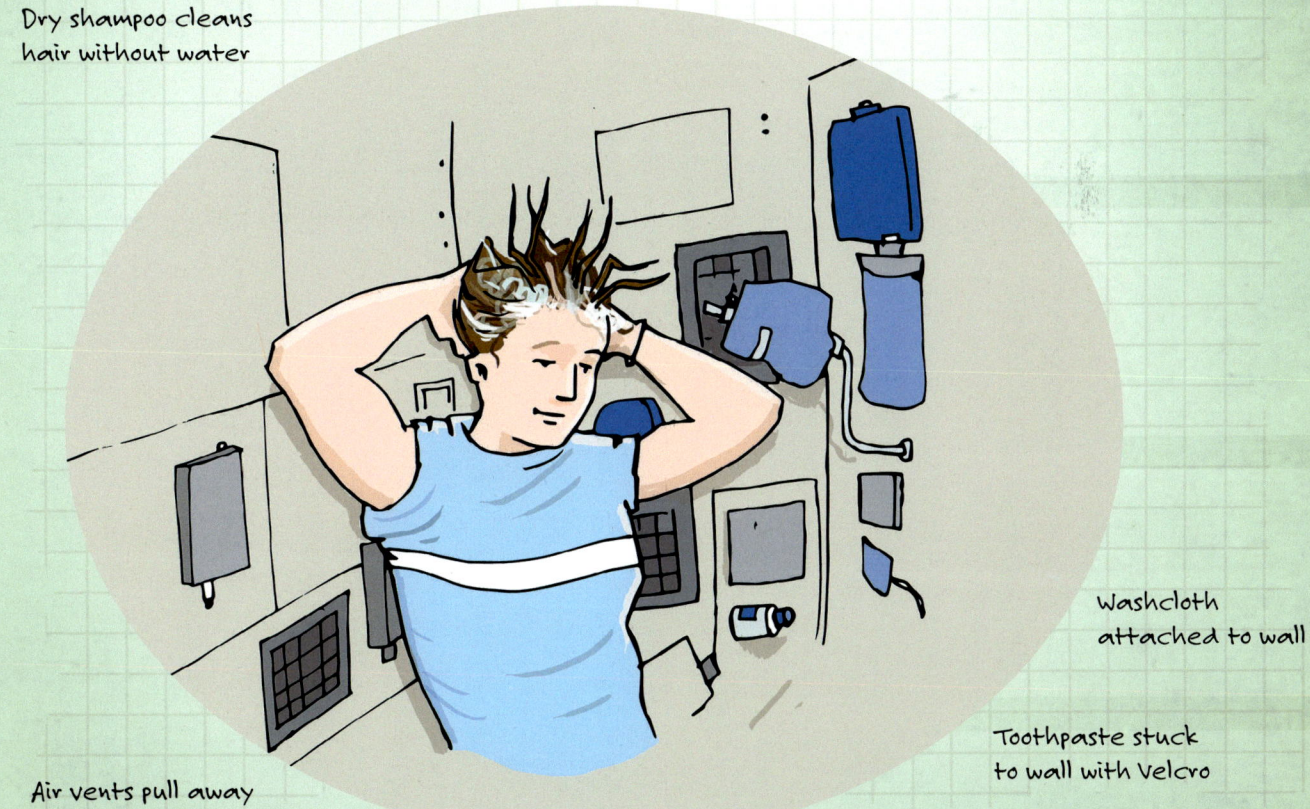

Dry shampoo cleans hair without water

Air vents pull away droplets of fluid

Washcloth attached to wall

Toothpaste stuck to wall with Velcro

MAKE THE ASTRONAUTS A BED

The original design had very comfortable sleeping facilities. After a hard day's astronauting, the crew would have been able to tumble into their bunk bed for a sleep. The guest quarters were even more luxurious. Unfortunately, though, all that is going to have to change.

SLEEP REDESIGN

The sleeping facilities on the space station need a complete rethink. There are two main problems to overcome:

1) No one on board will feel gravity. If they went to sleep in a normal bed, they would float off. Crashing into a wall or banging your head on the toilet would make for a bad night's sleep. Some way of stopping this is needed.

2) On the smaller, less-expensive version of the space station there will be very little space. The beds have to be as small as possible.

WORK IT OUT!

How can the sleepers be kept from floating off and banging into things? Do some research into ways that sleepers are kept secure on Earth. Find out about:

- capsule beds
- portaledge camping
- baby swaddling
- mummy sleeping bags

Would any of these help sleeping astronauts stay put? You can check your ideas on page 31.

Sleeping standing up? But in space you don't feel gravity, so there is no 'up'!

THE FINAL DESIGN

There will be two kinds of bed aboard the space station:

1) For the crew, there will be six sleeping capsules. (Not everyone will be asleep all the time, so more than six people will be able to use capsules for sleeping.) They will be like human-sized cupboards with padded walls. There will be hardly any room for floating around. The capsules will be soundproofed and sealed against light. Inside it will be quiet and dark.

2) When the space station is busy, extra guests will be strapped to the wall in a sleeping bag. An eye mask will block out light, and earplugs will keep out noise. It is not going to be very luxurious, but it will save a lot of space.

Research Note

Humans need an average of 7–8 hours of sleep every 24 hours. Most people sleep best in darkness and quiet.

Nights do not last very long aboard a space station 400km above the Earth. It takes only 90 minutes to travel around the planet. The space station is in darkness for only half this time. So one 'night' lasts just 45 minutes.

Sleeping capsules have room to move but not much else.

DESIGN A SPACE GYM

Some of the crew could be spending months in space. Living without gravity for long periods has serious effects on the human body. One way to fight these is exercise – so your next job is to design a space gym.

SPECIAL REQUIREMENTS

A space gym has special requirements. You cannot just design a normal gym from Earth, but a bit smaller so it fits in the space station. Most exercise on Earth relies on gravity. Running, weightlifting, football, dance and basketball, for example, all require gravity. Just try imagining what they would be like without it.

Research Note

Spending time without gravity affects the human body:

• On Earth, gravity pulls blood towards our feet. In space this does not happen. Extra blood stays in your upper body – causing your face to puff up alarmingly for a while.

• After a few days, your face stops being puffy – but only because your body has started making less blood.

• With less blood to deal with, your heart beats more slowly, and starts to get weaker.

• Without the need to fight gravity, your muscles and bones get weaker – bones by about 1% per month, muscles up to 5% a week.

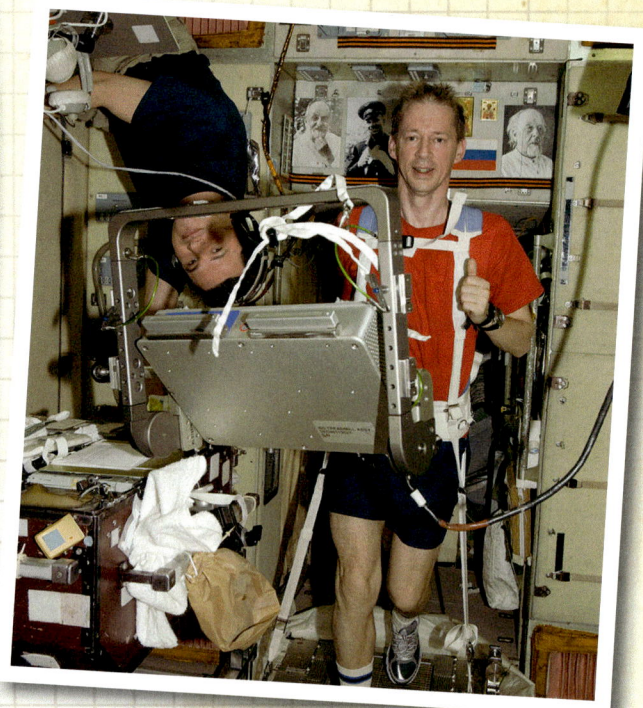

What would you call a mini gym like this one on board the International Space Station? A Foldaway Space Gym?

WORK IT OUT!

Can you come up with any kind of exercise that does not require gravity? Here are a few clues:

You might be able to find some that are not in the photos. Check your ideas on page 31, then sketch a gym that:

1) Does not take up much space

2) Allows astronauts to exercise every part of their body.

THE FINAL DESIGN

The final design is a gym that takes up hardly any space when it is not being used. Even so, it exercises the crucial parts of an astronaut's body. An exercise bike will give their heart and lungs a good workout. It will also help their leg muscles stay strong. (The rider will be strapped to the saddle so that she or he stays in place.) Stretchy bands attached to the walls will help the crew's leg, arm and body muscles. And finally, a boxing speed ball is there in case the astronauts feel like hitting something!

SCIENCE IN SPACE

The space station's original design was for a large science lab, in an area that did not have artificial gravity. In the new design, nowhere is going to have artificial gravity. The lab no longer needs its own area, and can be part of the main space station. Are any other changes needed?

Combustion research area

Fluids experiment area

Computer hard drives
Power unit
Air/heat recycling and control unit
Refrigeration and freezing

Materials research zone

Central computer workstations

Earth-research viewing/ recording window

Research Note

All kinds of special experiments can be done in a space station's microgravity. Many of them help scientists understand how we could one day make long-distance journeys through space.

1) Space flights are rocket powered, so we need to understand how combustion works in microgravity.

2) Long space flights would need to carry fuel in liquid form, so experiments with liquids are also useful.

3) Scientists need to experiment with how different materials behave in space.

4) How does microgravity affect living things – not only humans, but also animals?

As well as this, a space station has an amazing view from 400km up. It is able to record events on Earth, such as the spread of volcanic ash, which are not visible from the ground.

ESA astronaut Tim Peake unpacks the equipment he will use to carry out an experiment on board the ISS.

DESIGN CHALLENGES

The space station will now have to be much smaller than originally planned. The science lab will still have its own area – but now it will be about the size of an average room. So the biggest design challenge will be fitting everything in.

WORK IT OUT!

The new science lab will be just 2.5m across. But will everything that is needed fit inside this space?

These are the parts that have to be included, plus their sizes:

Combustion research area 100cm wide x 60cm deep	
Fluids experiment area	100 x 60
Materials research zone	90 x 70
Earth-research area and window	80 x 50
Computer workstations for each area	50 x 40
Power unit	90 x 50
Refrigeration and freezing	60 x 50
Air/heat recycling and control unit	90 x 60
Computer hard drives	50 x 50

To work out whether everything will fit, you need to know how big a circle is needed for them. If it is less that 2.5m across, everything will fit into the new lab.

Check your thinking on page 31.

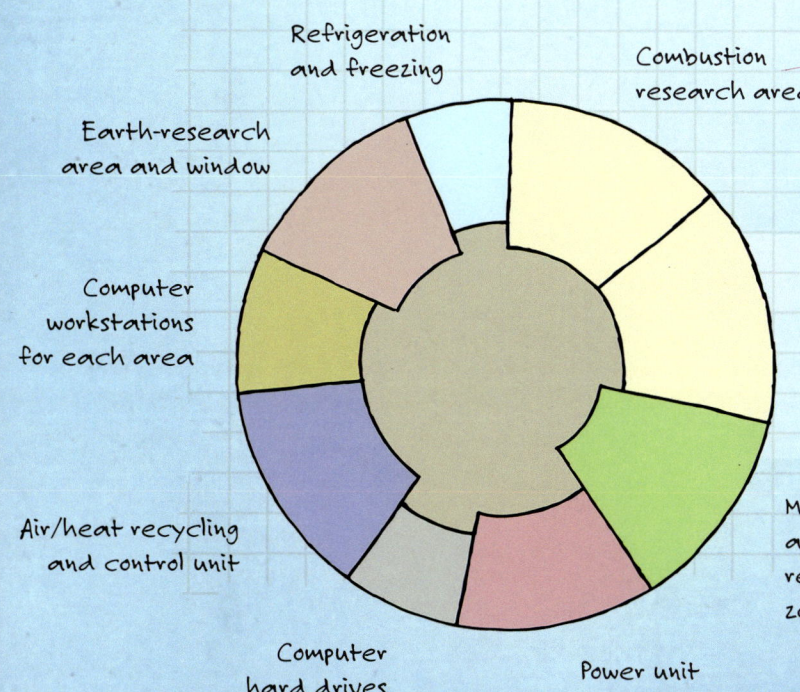

Refrigeration and freezing

Combustion research area

Earth-research area and window

Fluids experiment area

Computer workstations for each area

Materials and biology research zone

Air/heat recycling and control unit

Computer hard drives

Power unit

THE FINAL DESIGN

The final design is for a smaller lab inside the main space station. Even though it is smaller, it will still be able to do its job. The experiments done here will one day help us plan long-distance space flights.

THE BEST EVER SPACE STATION?

The financial crisis has meant some big changes for the space station design. It looks very different from the first drawing! But does the design still do everything it is supposed to? Does it fit the design brief?

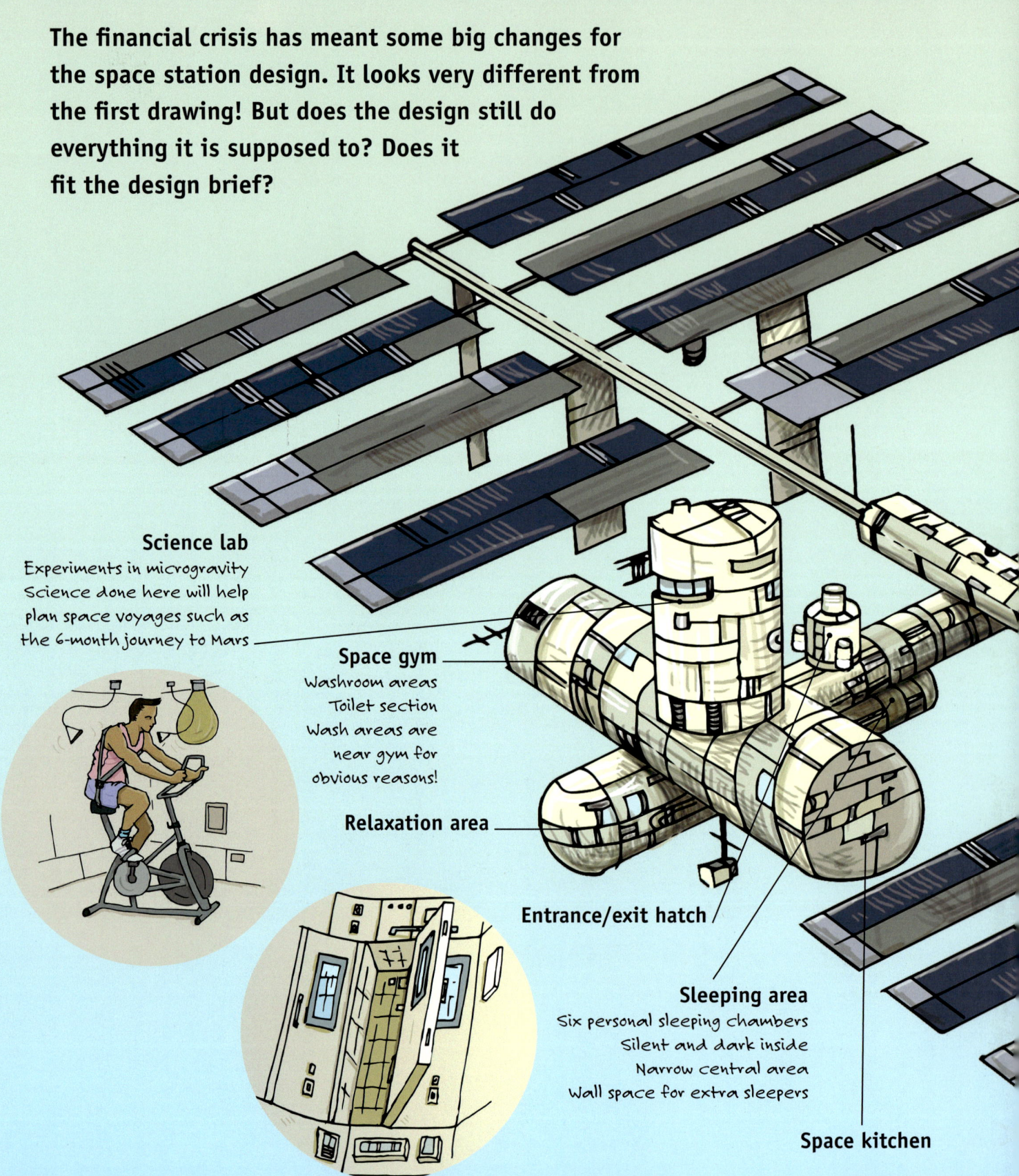

Science lab
Experiments in microgravity
Science done here will help
plan space voyages such as
the 6-month journey to Mars

Space gym
Washroom areas
Toilet section
Wash areas are
near gym for
obvious reasons!

Relaxation area

Entrance/exit hatch

Sleeping area
Six personal sleeping chambers
Silent and dark inside
Narrow central area
Wall space for extra sleepers

Space kitchen

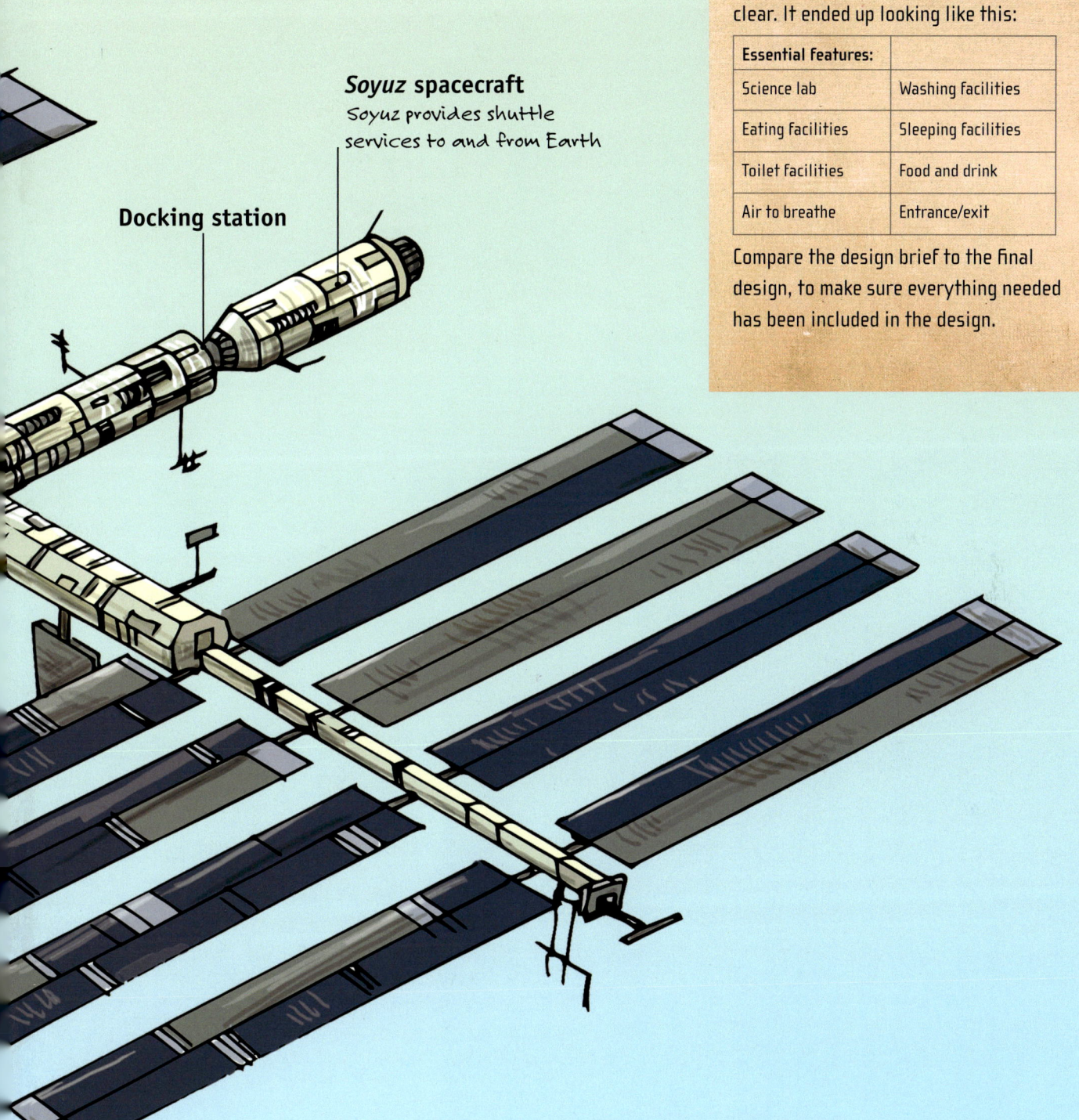

Docking station

***Soyuz* spacecraft**
Soyuz provides shuttle services to and from Earth

WORK IT OUT!

On page 9 of this book, the design brief for the space station became clear. It ended up looking like this:

Essential features:	
Science lab	Washing facilities
Eating facilities	Sleeping facilities
Toilet facilities	Food and drink
Air to breathe	Entrance/exit

Compare the design brief to the final design, to make sure everything needed has been included in the design.

OTHER SPACE STATIONS

People have been imagining what it would be like to live in space since at least the 1800s. In the 1950s scientists began sketching the first designs. Then, in the 1970s, the first space stations were actually built.

THE BRICK MOON

DESIGNED: 1869

The Brick Moon is a fictional space station. It appeared in a story in 1869. The Moon was meant to help with navigation, but was accidentally launched with people aboard. They survive, making them the first people ever to live on a space station (even if it was only an imaginary one).

SALYUT (USSR)

LAUNCHED: 1971

CRASHED/DISINTEGRATED: 1971

Salyut 1 was the first ever space station. It was also the first in a long line of Salyuts. In fact, Salyut technology is used aboard the International Space Station today.

SKYLAB (USA)

LAUNCHED: 1973

CRASHED/DISINTEGRATED: 1979

Skylab was the USA's first space station, and the first one to take account of astronaut comfort. Each crew member had a separate sleeping capsule, and there was a separate area for eating and relaxing.

MIR (USSR)

LAUNCHED: 1986

CRASHED/DISINTEGRATED: 2001

Mir (which is Russian for 'peace') was the first space station that was built in space. The central part was taken to space by rocket, then extra sections were added later. Three people were able to live aboard (more if they were not staying very long).

THE INTERNATIONAL SPACE STATION

LAUNCHED: 1998

CRASHED/DISINTEGRATED: Still operating

The cost of building and supporting space stations led the USA and Russia to work together to build the ISS. It is divided into American and Russian sections. Canada, the European Space Agency and Japan are also part of the ISS.

The International Space Station, currently in orbit somewhere above planet Earth.

'WORK IT OUT' ANSWERS

for p.5

yippy.com is a 'Deep Web' search engine, which visits pages most search engines do not reach. Its selection bar lets you narrow down research results by subject and source. duckduckgo.com has a different list of websites to Google, and orders the results in a different way.

for p.7

Your list for the day might look something like this. The items in italic are the non-essential activities:

07.45–07.47	Wake up; toilet (liquid)
07.47–08.00	Shower, clean teeth
08.00–08.20	Eat breakfast
08.20–08.45	*Travel on bus*
08.45–11.00	*Attend school/ study/work*
11.00–11.20	Have a drink, *play/relax* Toilet (liquid and solid)
11.20–13.00	*Attend school/ study/work*
13.00–13.45	Eat lunch, *play/relax*
13.45–15.45	*Attend school/ study/work*
15.45–16.00	*Travel on bus*
16.00–17.00	*Football practice;* toilet (liquid)
17.00–17.30	*Travel home*
17.30–18.15	Eat dinner
18.15–20.00	*Relax, watch telly*
20.00–20.15	*Argue about bedtime*
20.15–20.25	Clean teeth; toilet (liquid); get into bed
20.25–07.45	Sleep
All the time	Breathing

for p.9

Essential	Non essential
Science lab	Play area
Washing facilities	Football pitch
Eating facilities	School/office
Sleeping facilities	TV room
Toilet facilities	
Food and drink	
Air to breathe	
Entrance/exit	

for p.11

Skylab cost $100,000 per kg. *Mir* cost $5.6 billion, or $5,600,000,000. Divided among 100,000 kg, this gives a cost of $56,000 per kg. *International Space Station* cost $255,754 per kg. Space stations are very expensive to build.

for p.12

90 kilowatts is the most the space station will need. To add 15% for safety:

90 x 115 ÷ 100 = 103.5 kilowatts

Now divide this by 12.9 to work out how many solar panels are needed:

103.5 ÷ 12.9 = 8.02 solar panels.

for p.15

The best way for the astronauts to move between inside and outside will be an 'airlock' with two doors. They enter from one side and close the door. Then they open the other door to leave the airlock. This means the two atmospheres (the safe one inside the space station and the hostile one outside) only mix inside the airlock.

for p.17

The dropped pea is moving slowest and does least damage. The peashooter pea is moving fastest. Even though it is the same size as the other peas, it causes most damage.

for p.22

In a tiny capsule bed, the astronauts would not be able to drift off. Being attached like a climber on a portaledge would stop astronauts from floating away. Wrapping them up like a swaddled baby would not, and nor would mummy sleeping bags. A mummy sleeping bag attached to something would hold people in place while allowing them to move.

for p.25

The photos show (from left to right): 1) using an exercise bike; using stretchy bands to exercise your 2) arm and leg and 3) main body muscles; and 4) using a boxing speed ball (a leather ball that springs back into place when you hit it).

for p.27

Start by adding together the widths of all the units. These are:

100 + 100 + 90 + 80 + 50 + 90 + 60 + 90 + 50 = 710

How big would the circle be across, if it was this far around the outside? To work it out, divide the circumference (the outside-edge measurement) by a number called pi, which is usually simplified to 3.14. So:

710 ÷ 3.14 = 226

The circle would be 2.26m across, and the lab is actually 2.5m from side to side, so everything should fit.

GLOSSARY

adapted changed and made more suitable for its job

combustion burning something

design brief description of the most important things a product must do

estimate make a rough calculation

EVA short for 'extravehicular activity', which is anything done outside a space vehicle

fertiliser something added to soil to help plants grow

financial crisis shortage of money

g gravity: 1 g is the force of Earth's gravity as felt on Earth

habitable suitable for living in

labour cost of paying people to do work

material substance from which something can be made, such as metal or cotton

materials items that are used in a building or structure

microgravity force of gravity so small that it is almost impossible to detect

micrometeoroids tiny objects moving through space

nuclear fusion forcing two atoms together in a way that releases energy

orbit repeated path around a star or planet

reliable not likely to break down or malfunction

search engine tool for finding information on the Internet

solar panel device that turns sunlight into electricity

soundproofed made so that sound cannot get in

space tourism paying to visit space

USSR short for Union of Soviet Socialist Republics, a country based around Russia. The USSR existed between 1922 and 1991.

INDEX